11+ Maths

Year 4/5

Testpack A

(GL Assessment Style)

9781911553038

D1871935

Practice Paper 2

Please read the following before you start the Practice Paper:

1. Do not begin the Practice Paper until you are told to do so.
2. The Practice Paper contains 40 questions and you have 40 minutes to complete it.
3. Read the questions carefully so that you know what to do.
4. Try and answer as many questions as you can. Do not spend too much time on one question. If you cannot answer a question go on to the next one. If a question is omitted, ensure you have marked it clearly on your question paper, so it is easy to find it when you want to return to it after completing the rest of the paper.
5. If you are doing the Practice Paper as a standard test, write your answers clearly. If you want to change an answer, put a single line through the wrong answer and write the correct answer clearly.

   If you are doing the Practice Paper as a multiple-choice test, draw a clear line through your chosen box. If you want to change an answer, rub it out and mark the correct box clearly. **Do not write on or mark the answer sheet in any way other than that which has been specified.**
6. You may not use a calculator during this paper.
7. If you finish before your time ends, go back and check your answers.

Score	%
/40	%

1) The ratio of orange to water in a large jug of orange squash is 2 : 5

If 15 litres of water is used to make the drink, how much orange squash is used? 6 litres

2) Melanie has two 50 pence pieces, two 20 pence pieces, three 10 pence pieces and one 5 pence piece.

How much money does she have altogether? £1.75

3) Look at this list of numbers.

10 16 22 28 32 36 46 54 56 60

What percentage of the numbers are multiples of 4? 60 %

4) Eggs come in boxes of six.

How many whole boxes can be filled using 80 eggs? 13

5) What does the figure 4 represent in the number: 946,375?

A four hundred thousand

B four thousand

C four hundred

D forty thousand

E forty

D

6) Mr Kyle buys seven screws for 9 pence each.

How much change does he get from £1?

______ p

7) Basil was given the job of sorting out all the coloured pencils in the classroom.

The table shows how many of each colour he found.

Colour	Number of pencils
Red	25
Blue	?
Green	10
Yellow	20
Brown	25

If the mean is 20, how many blue pencils did he find?

______

8) This magic square adds up to 27 in all directions.

A		7
	9	
11	6	10

What is the value of A?

______

9) The parallelogram below has two angles marked.

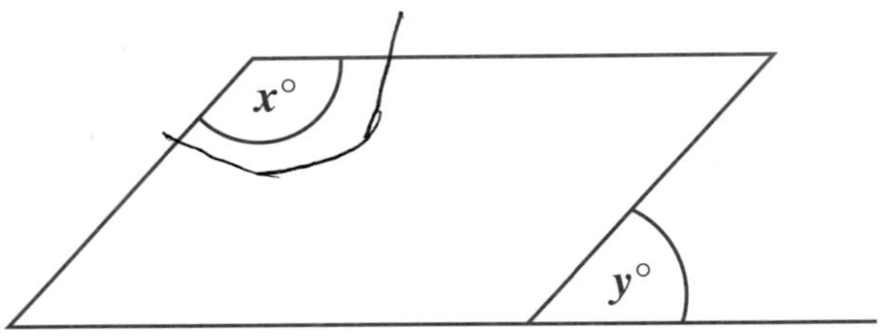

Angle y measures 65°.

What is the size of angle x? ______

10) Look at the list of numbers below:

9.9 10.05 9.59 10.1 9.97

Which of these numbers is closest to 10? ______

11) In the autumn the wind blows the leaves into a big pile outside the school entrance. One morning, Mr Baker's class gathers them up and separates them into types according to which type of tree they came from. They recorded their findings on a bar chart.

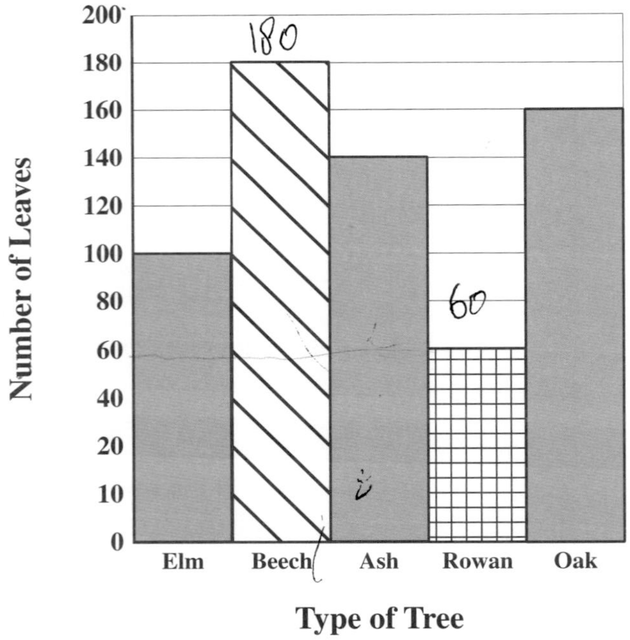

How many more beech leaves were there than rowan leaves? ______

12) Look at the expression below:

6^4

Which of the following answers represents exactly the same amount?

A 4×6

B $6 \times 6 \times 6 \times 6$

C $6 \times 4 \times 2$

D $6 + 6 + 6 + 6 + 6$

E $4 \times 4 \times 4 \times 4 \times 4 \times 4$

13) The spinner shown below has an equal chance of landing on any of the numbers.

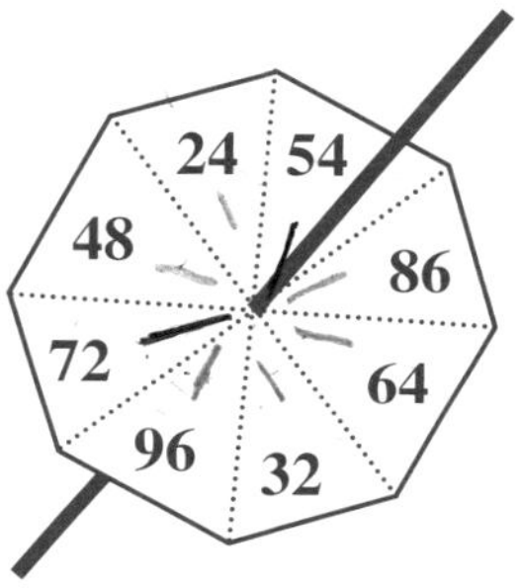

What is the chance that it will come to rest on a number that is a multiple of 9?

Write the answer as a fraction in its lowest possible terms.

14) 450 supporters turned up to watch a football match between United and Rangers.

There were 175 United supporters.

How many Rangers supporters were at the match?

15) Mrs Smedley bought a box of birthday cards to sell in her corner shop. When she opened the box, she found that $^{2}/_{3}$ of the cards were Christmas cards.

Altogether, there were 27 birthday cards.

How many cards were in the box in total?

16) In a year's time Susan will be twice as old as Mary was last year.

Mary is 8 years old.

How old is Susan now? ______

17) This is a floor plan of Miss Roger's classroom.

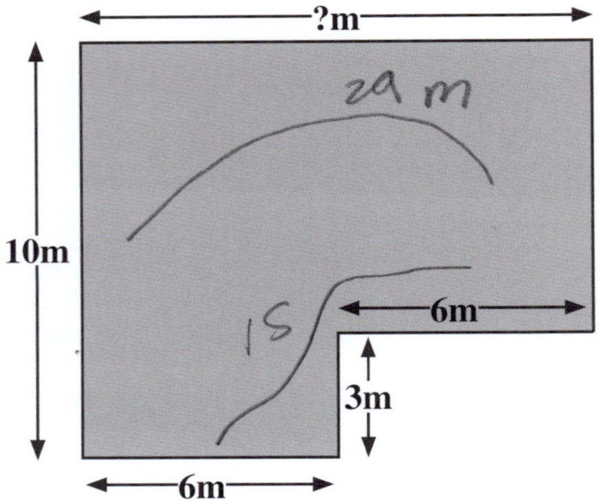

What is the total perimeter of the room? ______m

18) Which of the numbers below has the lowest value?

A 15.099 B 15.059 C 15.155 D 15.095 E 15.905 ______

19) Look at the graph below.

A, **B**, **C** and **D** mark the four corners of a rectangle.

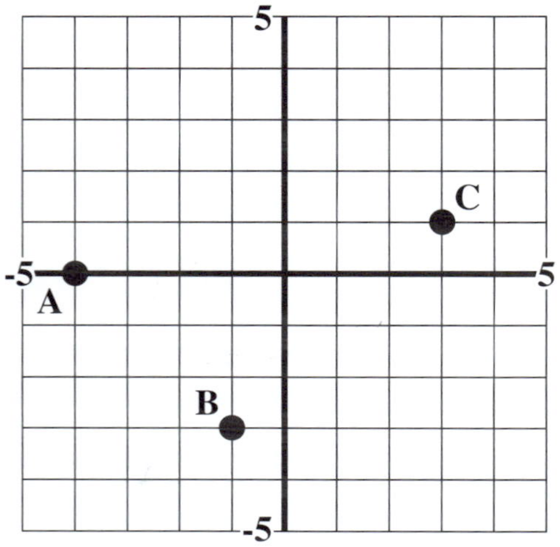

What are the co-ordinates of the missing point **D**? (____, ____)

20) Charlotte Sibley makes up crosswords for magazines and newspapers.

One year she created 25 big crosswords.
The next year she created twice as many.
During the following year she created twice as many as she had in the previous year.
How many crosswords did she create altogether in the three years?

____

21) Which of the following numbers is the only one that is divisible by both 3 and 7?

30 70 42 28 62

____

22) Look at the electronic weighing scales below.

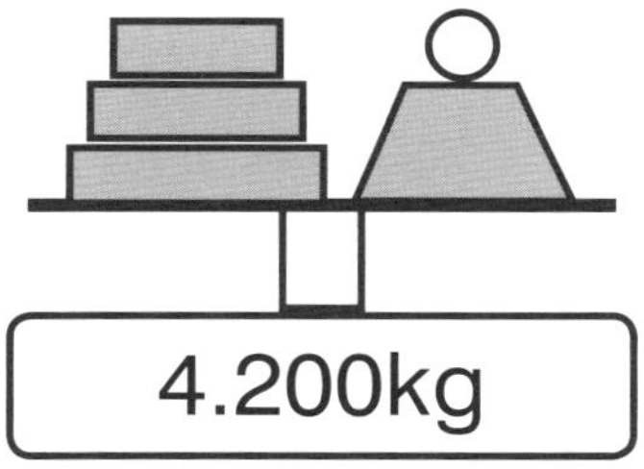

Duncan places some weights on the electronic scale.
He needs to make a total of 5kg.

Which two of the weights below should he choose to make up the weight to the correct amount?

A 325g B 575g C 450g D 375g E 475g ________ & ________

23) Mark and Jenny walk to and from school every day.
On Saturdays they go in the car with Mum to the supermarket.
On Sundays they walk to Grandma's house and back again.
The school is 2 miles away, Grandma lives 3 miles away and the supermarket is 5 miles away.

How far do the children each walk in a week? ________ miles

24) In a school with 150 pupils, 30 belong to the school choir.

What percentage of the school pupils are in the choir? ______ %

25) What is 161,579 rounded to the nearest hundred? ______

26) The Venn diagram below shows how many children in Mr Booth's class eat oranges or bananas or both.

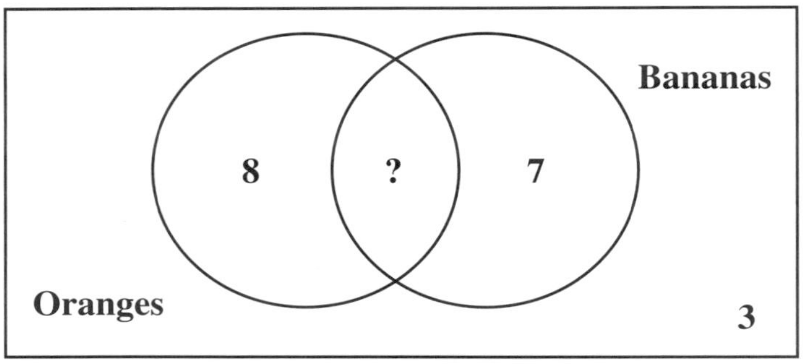

There are 30 children in Mr Booth's class. 3 children eat neither oranges or bananas.

How many children in the class eat both oranges and bananas? ______

27) Which of the following shapes cannot be drawn without lifting the pencil from the page or going over a line twice?

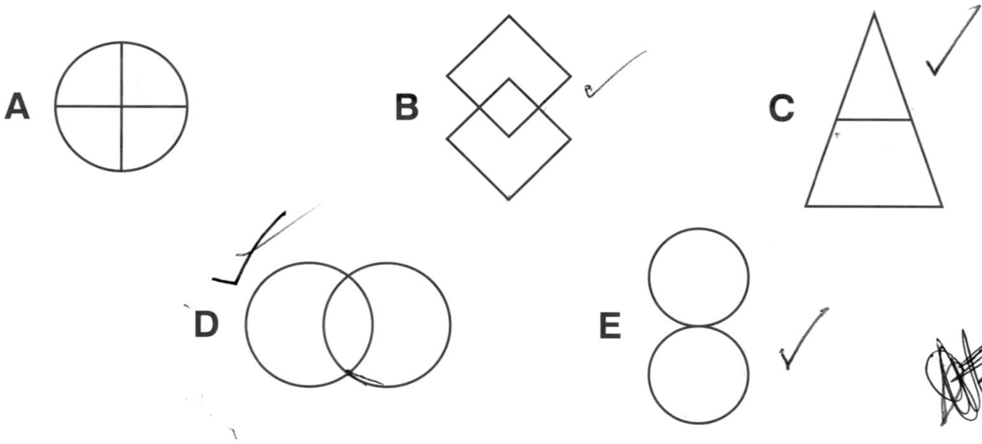

______

28) Look carefully at the grid below.

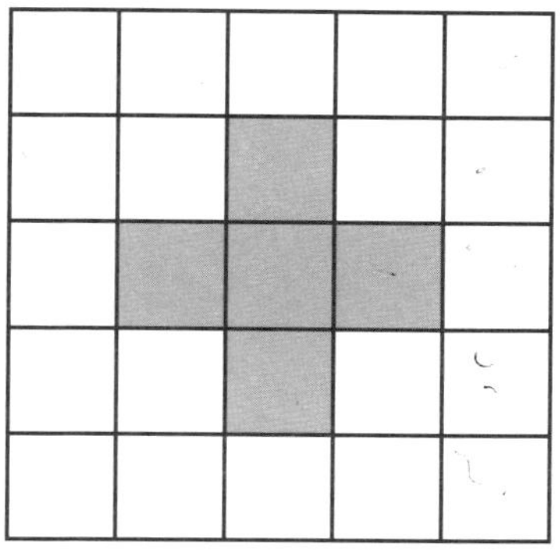

What fraction of this grid has been shaded?

Write the answer in its lowest possible terms. 1/5

29) A company makes packets of football cards.
Each pack contains 6 cards.

How many packs can be made from a pile of 96 cards? 16

30) Mum has £20.00 in her purse.
She spends £11.30 in the supermarket.

How much is left in her purse? £8.70

31) A survey was carried out to discover how many people bought cheese sandwiches in the railway station café.

Sales of Cheese Sandwiches	
Monday	■■■■▲▲●●
Tuesday	■■■▲●●
Wednesday	■■■▲▲●
Thursday	■■■■▲●
Friday	■■▲●●

KEY: ■ **10** people
▲ **3** people
● **1** person

How many sandwiches were sold on Wednesday? 37

32) Which of the following has the largest value?

A 10% of 100

B 50% of 40

C 75% of 20

D 20% of 30

E 25% of 60

______

33) Look at the number line below.

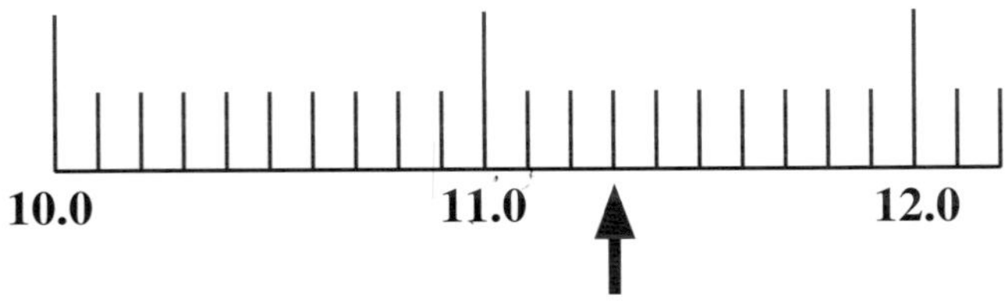

What is the value of the number that the arrow is pointing to? ______

34) Look at the net below. When folded it makes a box.

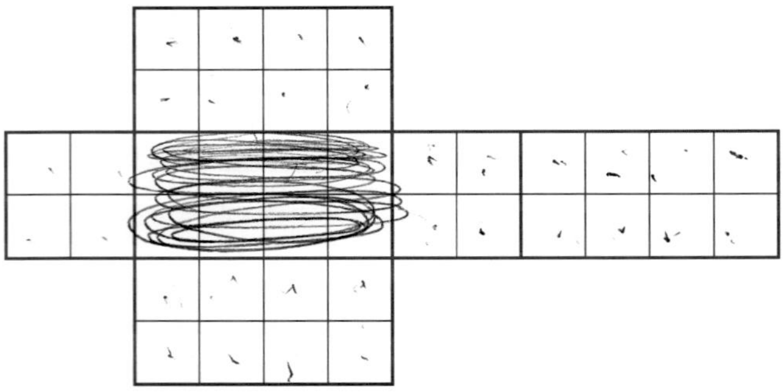

If the side of each small square is 1cm, what will be the total surface area of the box? ______ cm^2

35) Look at the following equation.

If $6x + 1 = 25$, what will $10x$ equal? ______

36) Ben spent £12.00 on figures for his model railway at the model shop. He bought 20 figures.

How much did each figure cost?

______ p

37) This is a map of part of a shopping centre. Find the way from the Entrance to the Café using a set of instructions.

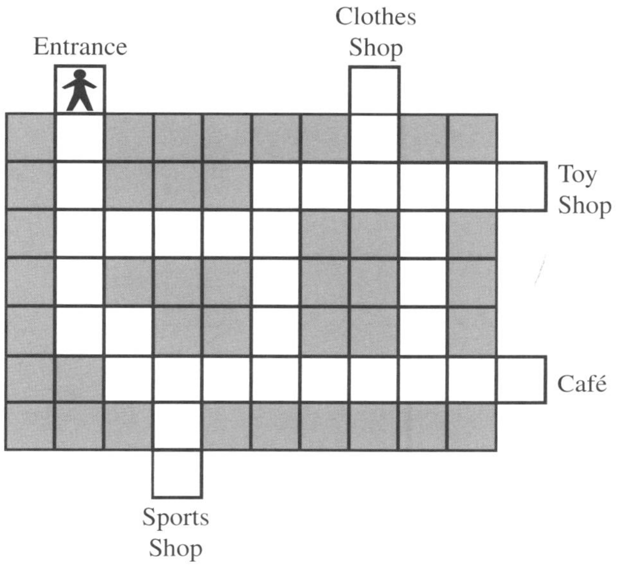

Key: FD means forward
RT means turn right 90°
LT means turn left 90°

Which of these is the only set of instructions that will lead to the Café?

A FD 3, LT, FD 4, LT, FD 1, RT, FD 5.

B FD 3, RT, FD 4, LT, FD 3, RT, FD 5.

C FD 5, RT, FD 1, LT, FD 6, RT, FD 1.

D FD 5, LT, FD 1, RT, FD 1, LT, FD 2.

E FD 3, LT, FD 4, RT, FD 3, LT, FD 5.

______

38) Look at the grid below.

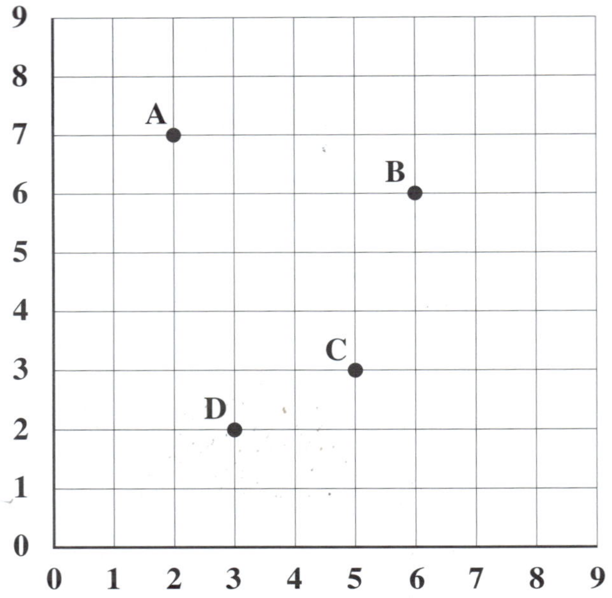

What are the co-ordinates of **A** and **C**?

	A	C
A	(2, 7)	(3, 5)
B	(7, 2)	(5, 3)
C	(5, 3)	(2, 7)
D	(7, 2)	(3, 5)
E	(2, 7)	(5, 3)

D

39) Highlighter pens cost 75 pence each.

How much will 6 pens cost?

75
6 ×
380

£ 3.80

40) Complete the following equation:

$10 \times 3 + 20 = 4 \times 7 + ?$ 22

22

Friday 26th of April Mock Exam
4:15 – 6:45

NVR
VR

END OF PAPER

11+ Maths

Year 4/5

Testpack A

(GL Assessment Style)

Practice Paper 3

Please read the following before you start the Practice Paper:

1. Do not begin the Practice Paper until you are told to do so.
2. The Practice Paper contains 40 questions and you have 40 minutes to complete it.
3. Read the questions carefully so that you know what to do.
4. Try and answer as many questions as you can. Do not spend too much time on one question. If you cannot answer a question go on to the next one. If a question is omitted, ensure you have marked it clearly on your question paper, so it is easy to find it when you want to return to it after completing the rest of the paper.
5. If you are doing the Practice Paper as a standard test, write your answers clearly. If you want to change an answer, put a single line through the wrong answer and write the correct answer clearly.

   If you are doing the Practice Paper as a multiple-choice test, draw a clear line through your chosen box. If you want to change an answer, rub it out and mark the correct box clearly. **Do not write on or mark the answer sheet in any way other than that which has been specified.**

6. You may not use a calculator during this paper.
7. If you finish before your time ends, go back and check your answers.

Score	%
/40	%

Answers

Exercise 1: 10

1) blunt
2) cowardly
3) eat
4) stupid
5) accompanied
6) sensible
7) careless
8) costly
9) uninterested
10) present

Exercise 1: 11

1) nurse
2) field
3) watch
4) charge
5) patch
6) grave
7) close
8) heart
9) fool
10) port

Exercise 1: 12

1) bitter
2) soil
3) content
4) notice
5) gentle
6) capture
7) match
8) present
9) bright
10) sort

Chapter Two
Cloze

Exercise 2: 1

1) Swimming, friends, pool
2) Before, packed, suitcase
3) restaurant, table, menu
4) campers, tent, fire
5) learn, practise, day
6) dinosaurs, fierce, tall
7) sport, team, Cup
8) tallest, located, south
9) carrying, world, shoulders
10) wings, many, quickly

Exercise 2: 2

1) often
2) apart
3) inventor
4) began
5) send
6) help
7) most
8) world
9) today
10) death

Exercise 2: 3

1) first
2) visit
3) name
4) born
5) king
6) helped
7) another
8) peace
9) brave
10) ocean

Exercise 2: 4

1) ruled
2) six
3) known
4) before
5) king
6) shortest
7) only
8) longest
9) monarch
10) famous

Exercise 2: 5

1) first
2) site
3) been
4) by
5) each
6) Three
7) with
8) over
9) is
10) since

Exercise 2: 6

1) born
2) family
3) played
4) child
5) very
6) later
7) world
8) known
9) other
10) won

Answers

Chapter One
Classification

Exercise 1: 1
1) metre
2) lion
3) plane
4) car
5) school
6) Germany
7) Tuesday
8) butterfly
9) banana
10) shop

Exercise 1: 2
1) twist
2) wage
3) window
4) train
5) read
6) joy
7) gnaw
8) permit
9) match
10) many

Exercise 1: 3
1) straight
2) big
3) earth
4) usual
5) sad
6) curtain
7) good
8) past
9) happy
10) plastic

Exercise 1: 4
1) talking
2) person
3) slow
4) fits
5) type
6) smile
7) aged
8) survivor
9) Autumn
10) mirror

Exercise 1: 5
1) dash
2) phantom
3) field
4) gutter
5) coast
6) serious
7) match
8) fury
9) servant
10) reply

Exercise 1: 6
1) famous
2) infant
3) glance
4) brush
5) troops
6) giggle
7) pause
8) harbour
9) scare
10) cooker

Exercise 1: 7
1) ruin
2) teacher
3) round
4) pirate
5) healed
6) start
7) tear
8) clown
9) weird
10) terrific

Exercise 1: 8
1) crouch
2) below
3) capture
4) warm
5) admit
6) serious
7) penniless
8) few
9) lower
10) repair

Exercise 1: 9
1) absent
2) polite
3) right
4) loose
5) narrow
6) groan
7) attack
8) import
9) heavy
10) ignore

1) This is a plan of the school car park.

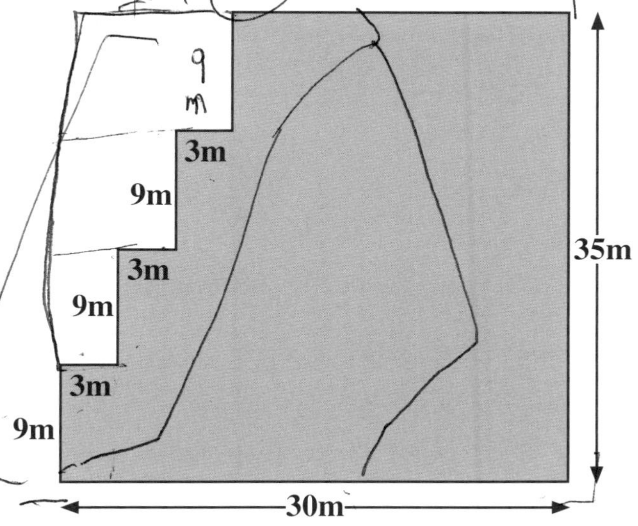

What is the perimeter of the car park? ______ m

2) This spinner has an equal chance of landing on any of the numbers.

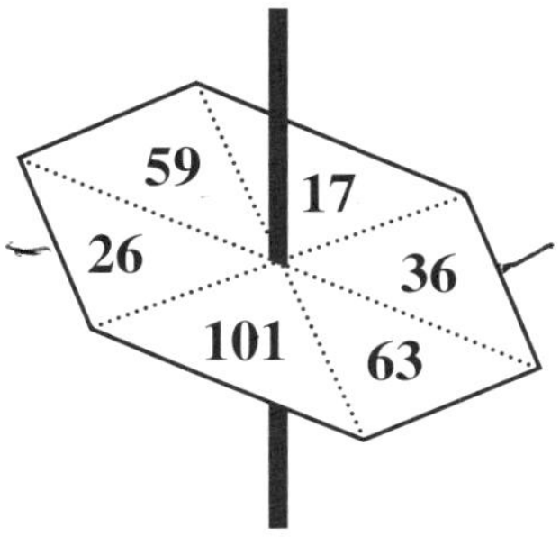

What is the chance that it will come to rest on an even number?

Write the answer as a fraction in its lowest possible terms. ______

3) Mr Ivanovich sells fireworks in his shop during the week before bonfire night in November.

The bar chart below shows how many fireworks of different types he sold on the 5th of November.

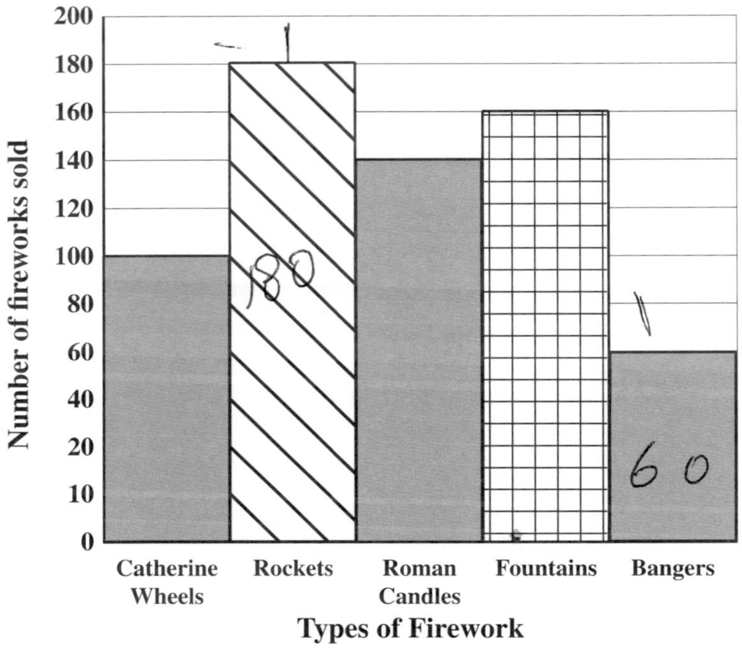

How many Rockets and Bangers were sold altogether? ______

4) Look at the equation below.

$5a - 12 = 28$

What is the value of a?

A 7

B 6

C 5

D 9

E 8

______

5) Mrs Bailey's class use a decision tree to sort some paper in the classroom.

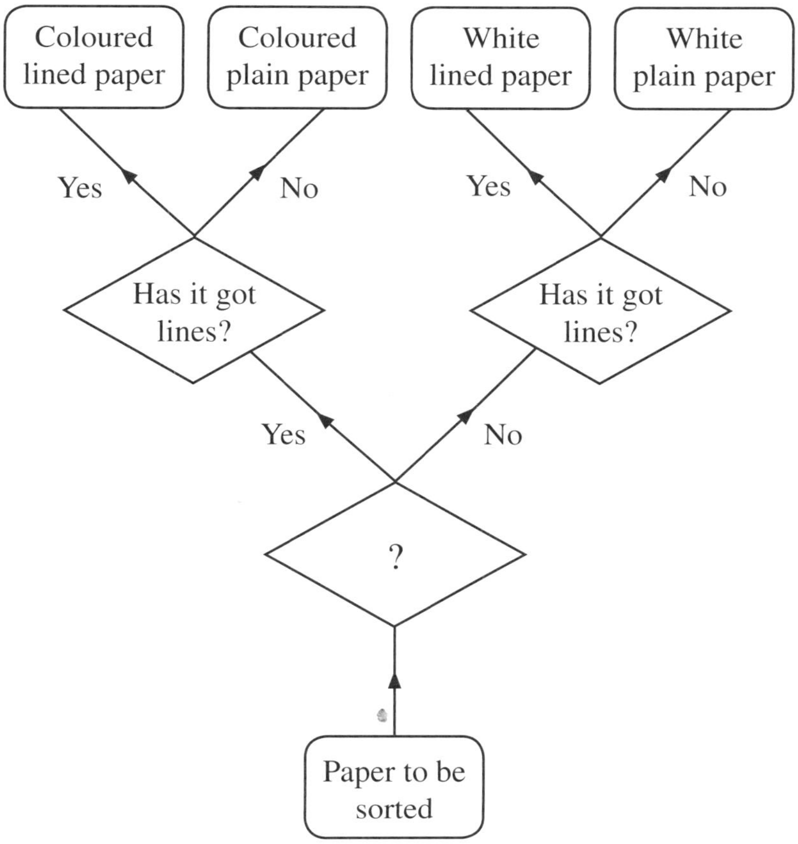

What words are missing from the empty box?

A Is this paper green?

B Is this paper A4 size?

C Has it got writing on it?

D Is this paper coloured?

E Is this paper lined?

6) $6^2 = ?$

A 36

B 12

C 18

D 64

E 8

7) Which one of the following five letters has two lines of symmetry?

A **C** B **O** C **A**

D **T** E **S**

______

8) It snowed every day last week.

This table shows how many centimetres of snow fell on each day.

Day	cm of snow
Mon	19cm
Tues	15cm
Wed	19cm
Thurs	11cm
Fri	?

The mean is 16.

How many centimetres of snow fell on Friday? ______ cm

9) Chris bought five packets of mints.

He was given 30 pence change from £1.

How much did each packet cost? ______ p

10) The following pictograph shows how many milkshakes were sold in the school canteen each day last week.

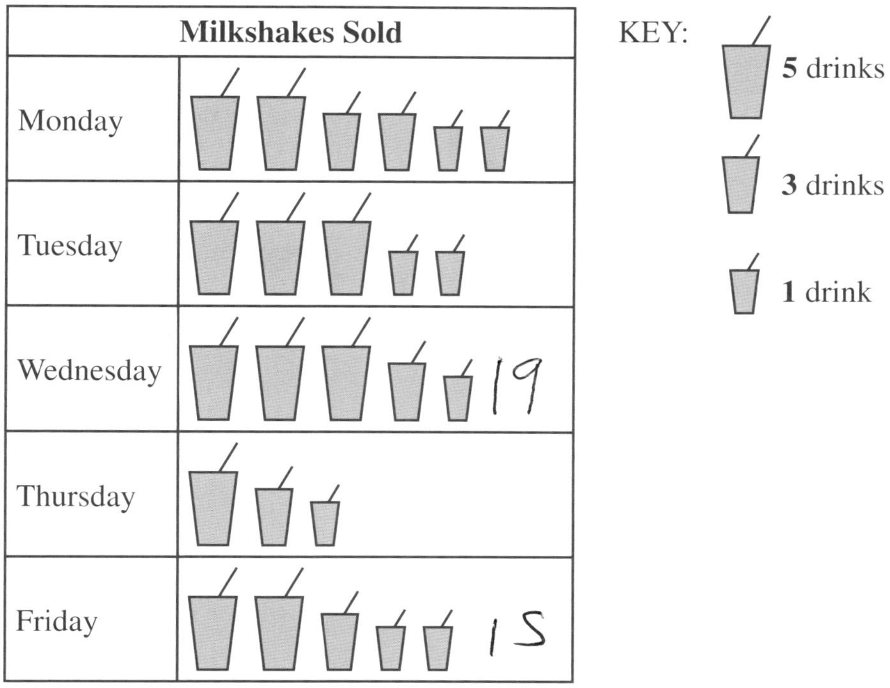

How many milkshakes were sold altogether on Wednesday and Friday?

11)

8	17	26
17	26	35
26	35	?

What is the missing number on this grid?

12) Look at the number line below.

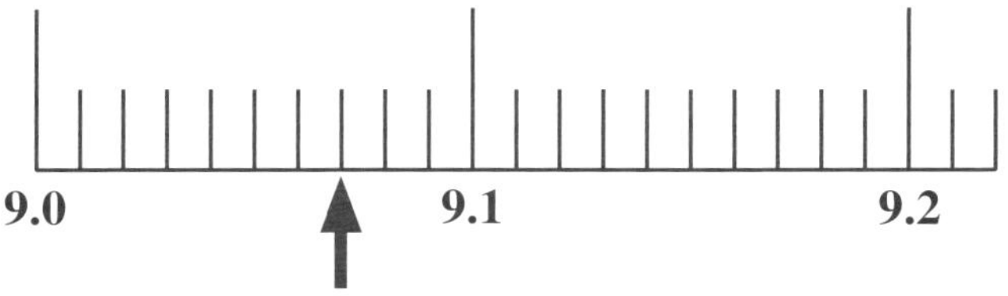

What is the value of the number that the arrow is pointing to?

13) How many faces are there on a tetrahedron?

14) The ratio of flour to sugar in a cake mix is 5 : 3.

If 150g of sugar was used to make the cake, how much flour was used? ______

15) Find the missing number in the equation below.

$(10 \times 2) + 5 = (? \times 3) + 7$ 6

16) In a packet of 20 balloons, 8 are red and the remainder are blue.

What fraction are blue?

Write the answer in its lowest possible form. ______

17) Look at the diagram below.

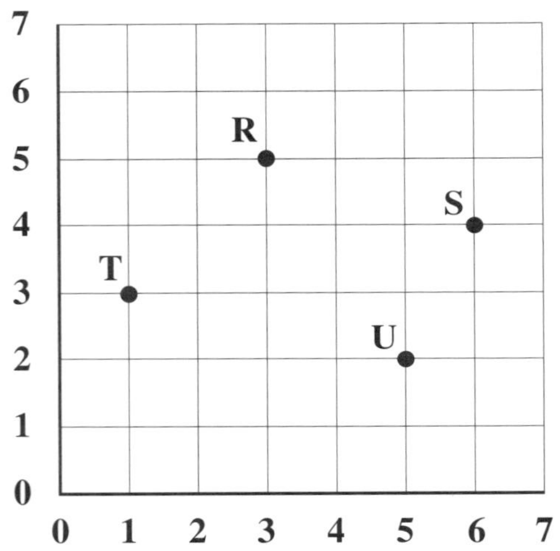

What are the co-ordinates of the points at letter **U** and letter **T**?

U: (2, 5)   T: (3, 1)

18) If a number is multiplied by itself and then 10 is added, the new number is 46.

What is the original number? 6

19) This is a map of Mary's bungalow.

Find the way from the Front Door to Bedroom 1 using a set of instructions.

Key: FD means forward
RT means turn right 90°
LT means turn left 90°

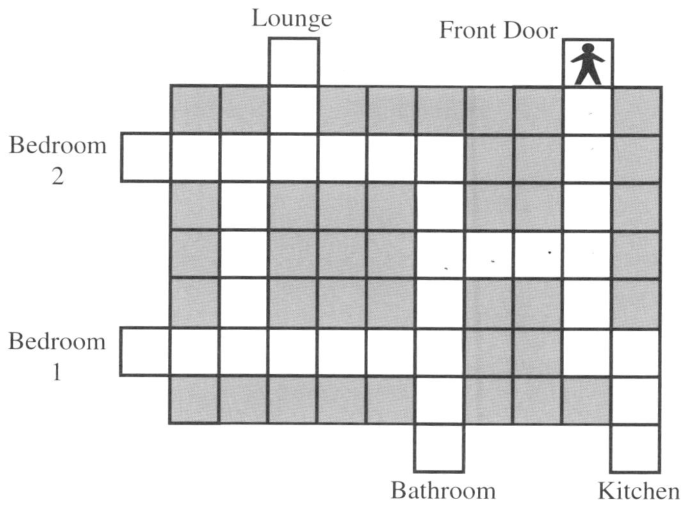

Which of these sets of instructions is the correct one?

A FD 4, LT, FD 4, RT, FD 3, RT, FD 2.

B FD 4, RT, FD 3, LT, FD 2, RT, FD 6.

C FD 4, LT, FD 3, RT, FD 3, RT, FD 6.

D FD 3, RT, FD 3, LT, FD 2, RT, FD 2.

E FD 4, RT, FD 4, LT, FD 2, RT, FD 6.

20) The cost of 12 eggs is x pounds.

What will the cost of three eggs be?

A $x \div 4$

B $x \div 12$

C $y \times 3$

D $x \div 3$

E $x - 9$

21) Which one of these shapes has no lines of symmetry?

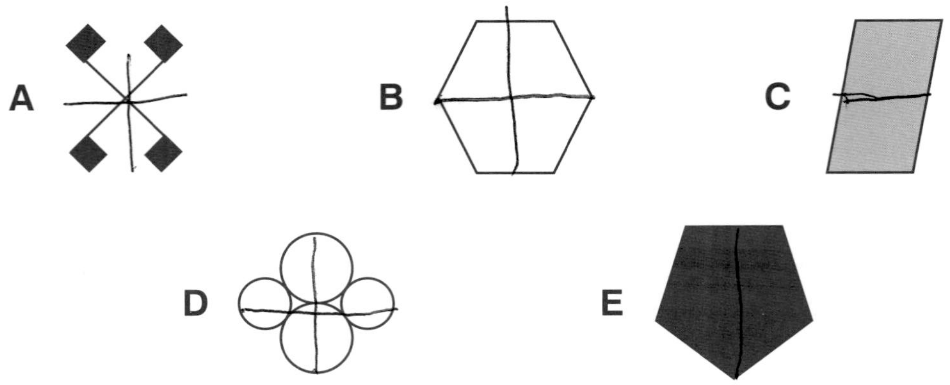

22) 353 people travelled to Spain on an aeroplane.
165 of them were adults and the remainder were children.

How many children were on the aeroplane?

23) In the local burger bar, a large cardboard cup of cola contains the same amount as 3 small cups.

Four of the following combinations contain the same amount of cola.

Which one contains a different amount?

A 2 large, 6 small

B 3 large, 3 small

C 4 large, 0 small

D 3 large, 2 small

E 1 large, 9 small

24) A rectangle has one pair of sides which are each 10cm in length.
The total area of the rectangle is $30cm^2$.

How long are each of the other two sides?

A 20cm

B 3cm

C 15cm

D 5cm

E 8cm

25) The table below shows how much time it takes to cook different foods.

Food	Time taken to cook
Large Cake	50mins
Lasagne	1hr 20mins
Toad in the Hole	45m
Vegetarian Stew	2hrs 45mins
Roast Turkey	3hrs

What is the ~~range?~~ what is a range ____hrs ____mins

26) Dave's mum buys him a new coat.
It has been reduced by 50% in the sale.
The original cost was £48.50.

How much did the coat cost her? £ 24.25p

27) How should 6.15 in the evening be written in 24-hour clock?

A 6.15am

B 06:15

C 6.15pm

D 16:15

E 18:15

E

28) Which of the following numbers is divisible by both 4 and 5?

~~10~~ ~~30~~ ~~50~~ ~~70~~ 80

80

29) A company that makes birthday cards sends 70 boxes to a shop.
Each box contains 60 cards.

How many birthday cards did it send in total? 4200

30) Vinnie is paid £5 per week to wash his father's car.
How many weeks will it take him to earn enough money to buy a printer costing £72.50?

31) Which group contains only square numbers?

A 36 25 81 50 16

B 21 35 55 64 100

C 54 25 36 100 18

D 40 121 81 49 100

E 49 4 64 36 25

32) Look at this list of numbers:

-4 6 9 3 -8

What is the difference between the largest and smallest?

33) Which of the following shapes has one less face than it has vertices?

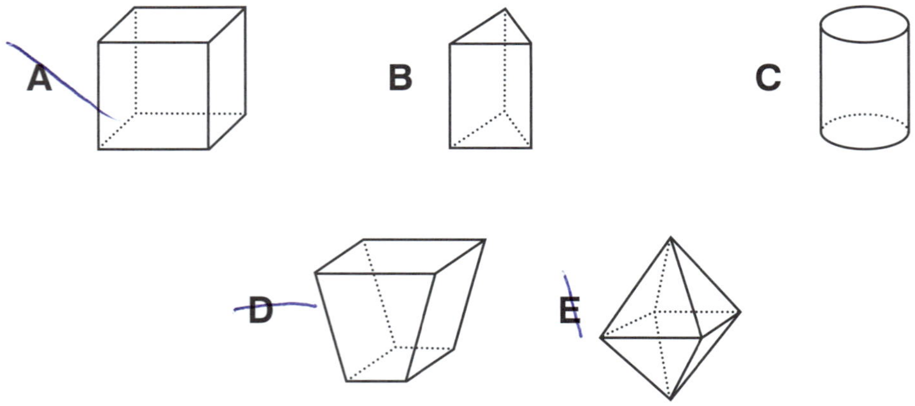

34) What is 6 multiplied by 9, then divided by 3?

35) Look at the diagram below:

Favourite TV Programmes	
Bottom Gear	☐☐■■■■
Red Peter	☐☐☐■■■
Z Factor	☐☐■■■ 13
Dr Which	☐☐☐☐■■ 22
Strongest Link	☐☐■

KEY: ☐ **5** children

■ **1** child

How many more children liked 'Dr Which' than liked 'Z Factor'? 9

36) The temperature in Birmingham, England, was -3°C yesterday. In Oslo, Norway, the temperature was -13°C.

What was the difference between the temperatures in Birmingham and Oslo? -10 °C

37) Look at the following groups of numbers.

Which group contains only multiples of 3 or 6?

A 6 18 27 30 46

B 9 24 36 54 76

C 12 30 46 93 120

D 24 48 63 70 102

E 30 51 60 69 72

E

38) In 3 years' time Ian will be twice as old as Monica is now. Monica is 9 years old.

How old is Ian? 15 years old

39) The pie chart below shows the results of a survey of which sport the pupils at Hilltop School prefer to play.

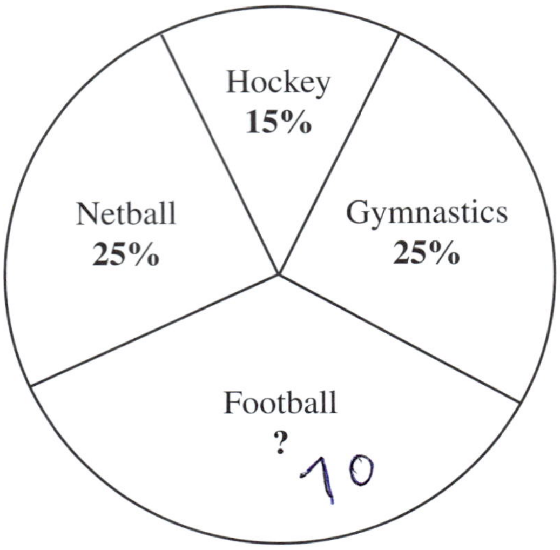

70 children said they prefer to play football.

How many children took part in the survey? ______

40) Calculate this sum:

$\frac{3}{4} - \frac{3}{8} =$ ______

END OF PAPER

Test 28

Maths - 11
Non-Verb - 6
Verbal - 19

11+ Maths

Year 4/5
Testpack A
(GL Assessment Style)

Practice Paper 4

Please read the following before you start the Practice Paper:

1. Do not begin the Practice Paper until you are told to do so.

2. The Practice Paper contains 40 questions and you have 40 minutes to complete it.

3. Read the questions carefully so that you know what to do.

4. Try and answer as many questions as you can. Do not spend too much time on one question. If you cannot answer a question go on to the next one. If a question is omitted, ensure you have marked it clearly on your question paper, so it is easy to find it when you want to return to it after completing the rest of the paper.

5. If you are doing the Practice Paper as a standard test, write your answers clearly. If you want to change an answer, put a single line through the wrong answer and write the correct answer clearly.

   If you are doing the Practice Paper as a multiple-choice test, draw a clear line through your chosen box. If you want to change an answer, rub it out and mark the correct box clearly. **Do not write on or mark the answer sheet in any way other than that which has been specified.**

6. You may not use a calculator during this paper.

7. If you finish before your time ends, go back and check your answers.

Score 31 / 40

% 84 %

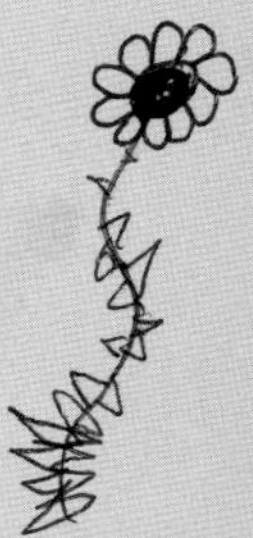

1) In two years' time Bernice will be the same age as her sister Annabel was last year.

Annabel will be 12 next birthday.

How old is Bernice now? ______

2) This function machine multiplies by 4 and then subtracts 9.

? → × 4 → − 9 → 27

What number went into the machine? ______

3) Look at the shape below.

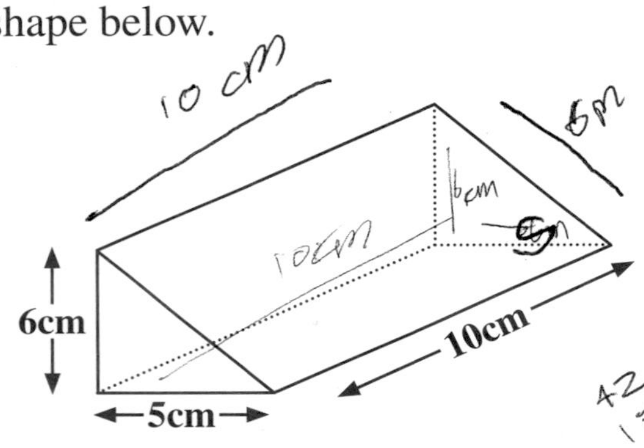

What is the volume of this shape? ______ cm^3

4) There are sixteen balls in a bag. Ten of them are red and six of them are blue.

Wendy puts her hand in the bag and pulls out a ball without looking.

What is the chance that Wendy will pull out a blue ball? ______

5) Sandy is a delivery driver for the local florist.

The table shows how many deliveries she made last week.

Day	Number of deliveries
Mon	9
Tues	8
Wed	?
Thurs	10
Fri	6

The mean is 9.

How many deliveries did she make on Wednesday? 12

6) Jamal bought 4 cardboard badges.
He was given 32 pence change from £1.

How much did each badge cost? 17 p

7) Look at the grid below.

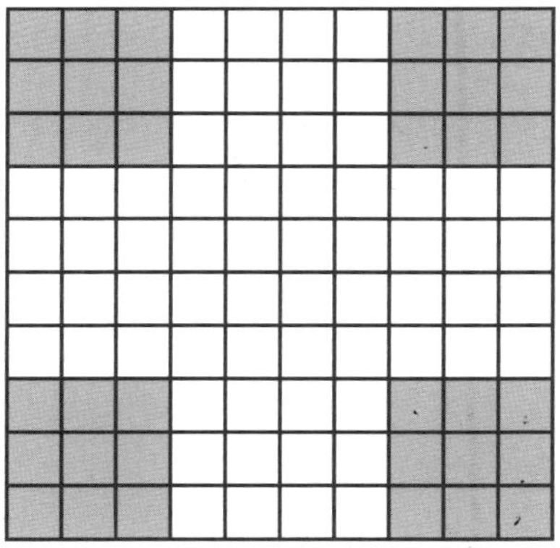

What percentage of the grid remains unshaded? 64 %

8) The hands of the classroom clock show the time 4 o'clock.
What is the smaller of the two angles between the minute hand and the hand hour? 120 °

9) Approximately how much liquid is found in a standard size can of cola?

3,000mℓ   0.03 litres   300cℓ

300mℓ   3cℓ

300ml

10) This is a floor plan of Mr Jones' office.

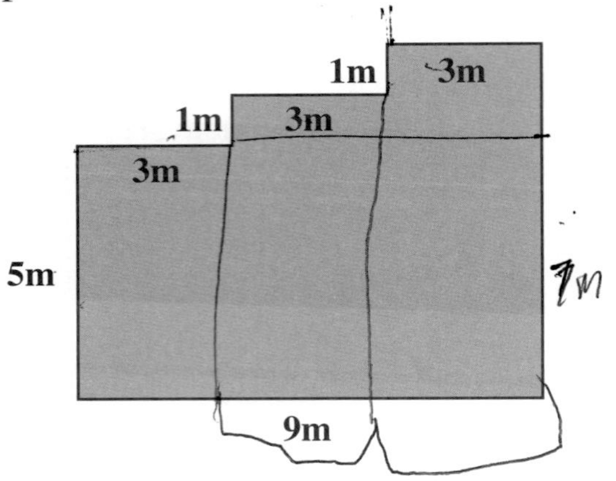

What is the total area of the floor? ______ m²

11) If $5x - 11 = (4 \times 4) + 28$,

what is the value of x? ______

12) This magic square adds up to 30 in all directions.

	7	9
A		
11	13	

What is the value of A? ______

13) In a box of 40 packets of crisps, 16 are chicken flavour and the remainder are salt and vinegar.

What fraction of the box are salt and vinegar? ______

14) If a number is multiplied by itself and the answer is multiplied by 3, the new number is 75.

What is the original number? ______

15) Look at the diagram below.

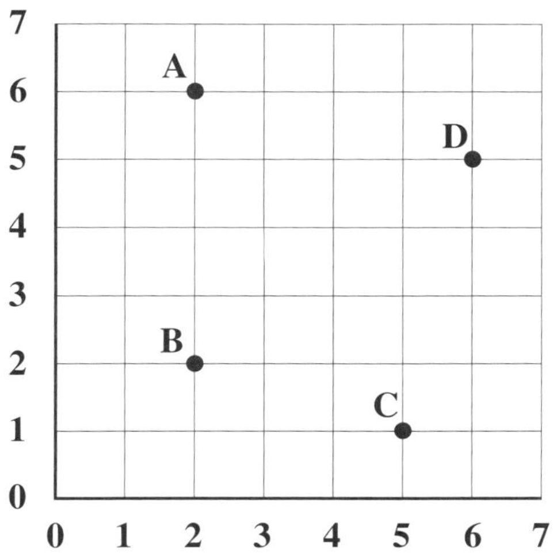

What are the co-ordinates of the points at letter **D** and letter **C**?

D: (5 , 6)   C: (1 , 5)

16) The temperature in Edinburgh, Scotland, was -9°C yesterday.
In Paris, France, the temperature was 14°C.

What was the difference between the temperatures in Edinburgh and Paris? 23 °C

17) Stephen is doodling with his pen.
He is drawing shapes.

Only one of the following shapes can be drawn without lifting his pen from the page or going over a line twice. Which one?

A 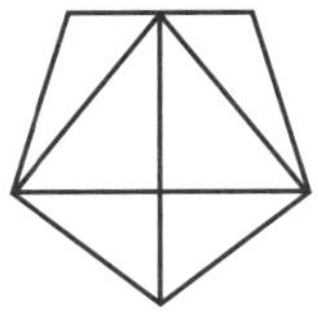

B 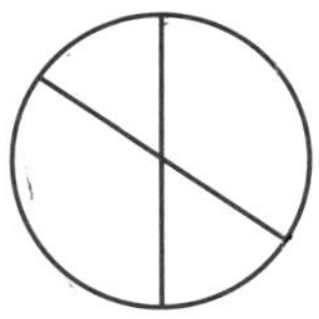

C 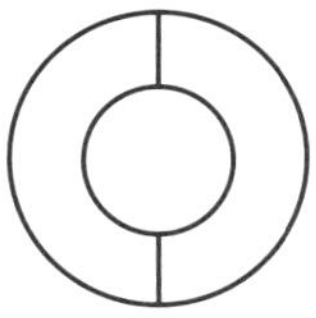

D 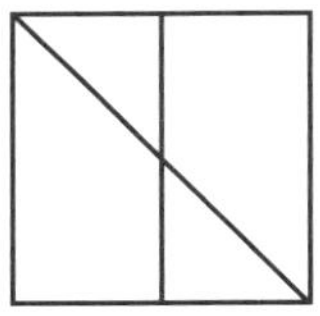

E 

A

18) How many minutes are there in 6 hours? 360 mins

19) This graph shows the conversion rate between UK pounds (£) and Australian dollars (Au$).

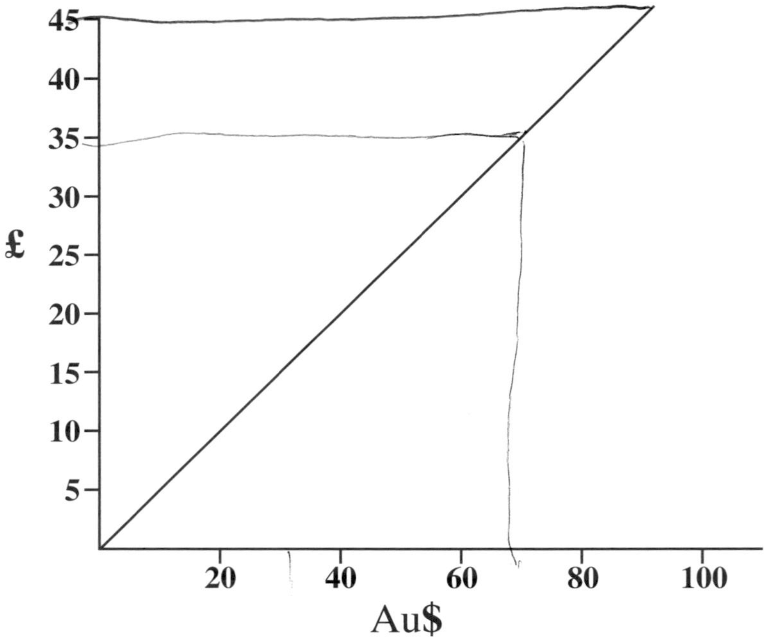

How many pounds would need to be changed to get 70 dollars? £35

20) This year Rebecca has taken seven maths tests.

Here are her results out of a possible 20:

15 19 8 13 11 9 16

What was her mean score? 13

21) If $x = 6$ and $y = 5$,

$2y + 4x$ = 34

22) Look carefully at the graph below.

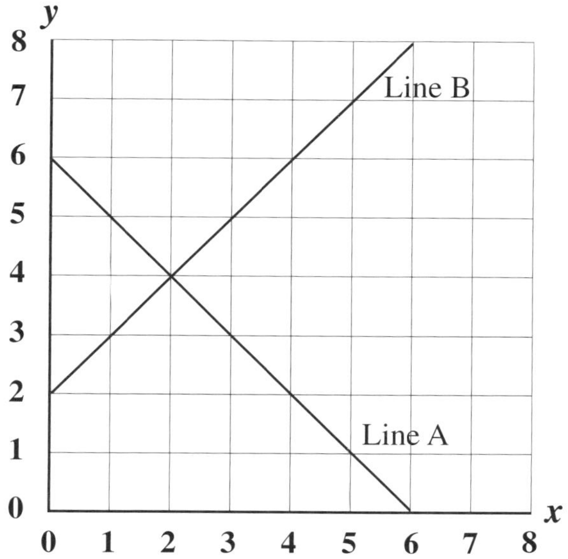

What is the rule that governs the plotting of Line B?

A $x = y + 2$

B $x = 2y$

C $2y = x$

D $y - 2 = x$

E $2x + 2 = y$

23) Look at the number line below.

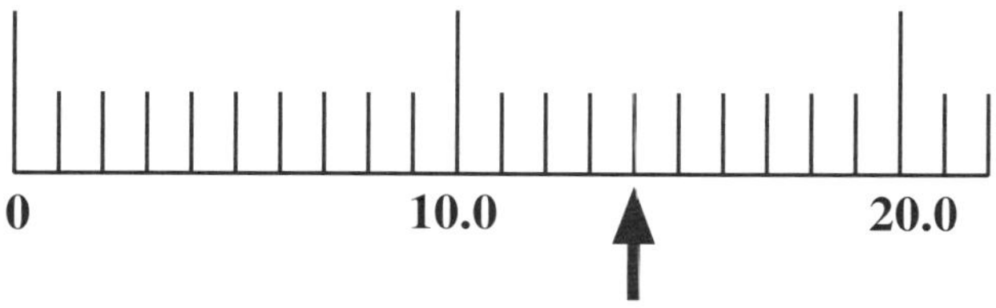

What is the value of the number that the arrow is pointing to? ______

24) Look at the shape below.

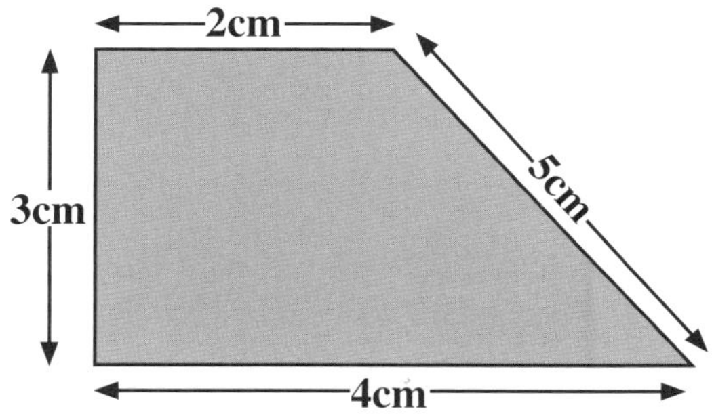

What is the total area of the shape? ______ cm^2

25) This spinner has an equal chance of landing on any of the numbers.

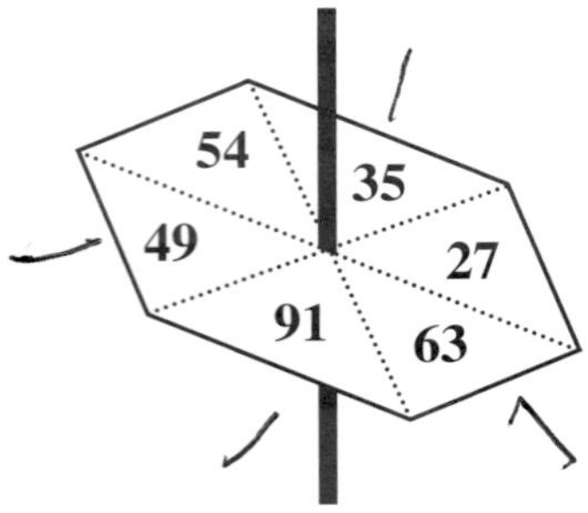

What is the chance that it will come to rest on a number that is a multiple of 7?

Write the answer as a fraction in its lowest possible terms. 2/3

26) A bicycle manufacturer makes a championship racing bike and sells it in several different colours.

The bar chart below shows how many bicycles were sold in one month.

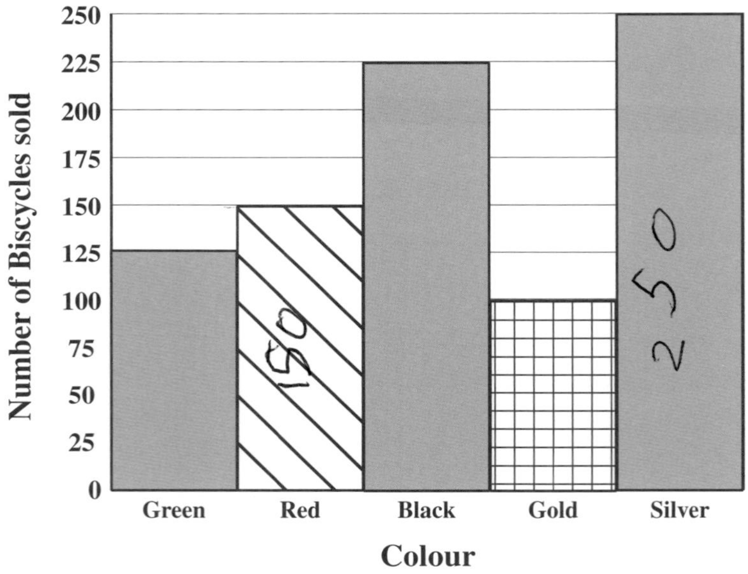

How many more silver bikes were sold than red bikes? 100

27) There are 35 children on a coach trip to London. 20 are girls and 15 are boys.

One child's name is chosen at random to collect the tickets.

What is the chance that the child will be a boy?

Give the answer as a fraction in its lowest terms. 3/7

28) Birmingham United played Newcastle City in a football match.

The match kicked off at 2.30pm. They played 45 minutes each half and had a half-time break of 15 minutes.

At what time did the match end? ________

29) The table below shows how much time Mr Knight spends marking books each day.

Day	Time spent marking books
Monday	1hr 15mins
Tuesday	$2\frac{3}{4}$hrs
Wednesday	2hrs 25mins
Thursday	90mins
Friday	$3\frac{1}{2}$hrs
Saturday	2hrs 45mins

What is the range? ____ hrs ____ mins

30) Kylie bought a pair of gold earrings.
They had been reduced by 20% in the sale.
The original cost was £6.00.

How much did the earrings cost her? £________

31) How would 9.45 at night be shown on a 24-hour clock?

A 9.45am

B 21:45

C 9.45pm

D 09:45

E 2145pm

____

32) Which of the following numbers is divisible by both 4 and 6.

38 26 18 56 48

______

33) Mrs Billings takes her daughter Sandy to the local market to buy some clothes.

She spends £28.50 on a jacket, £4.50 each for two T-shirts and £9.50 on a skirt for school.

How much did Mrs Billings spend?

£______

34) Judy is paid £8 each Saturday to help her father in his corner shop. How many weeks will it take her to earn enough money to buy a violin case costing £66?

______

35) 5^3 = ?

A 25

B 50

C 15

D 125

E 250

______

36) Look at the nets below.

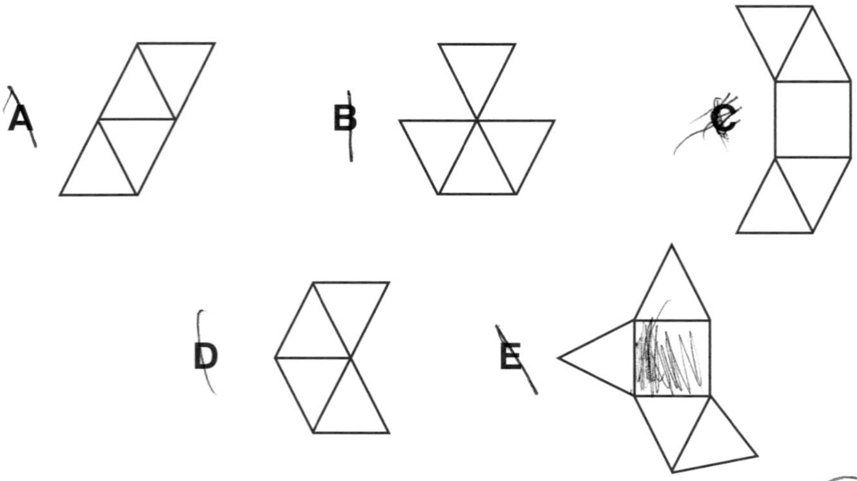

Which one of these nets will form a pyramid?

______

37) Complete the following number sequence:

2, 8, 20, 44, 92, 188, ? ______

38) Barbara gets £2 pocket money each week from her father.
She receives an extra £1 every day for helping with the washing up, feeding the cat and walking the dog.

How much money will Barbara receive in 4 weeks? £______

39) Mrs Bishop went to the local supermarket to buy some sausages.
In the shop there were 5 different packs of sausages at 5 different prices:

A Mighty Banger £4.50 / pack of 5

B Veggy Sausage £6.00 / pack of 15

C Family Pack £10.00 / pack of 25

D Sizzlers £8.00 / pack of 10

E Chipolatas £6.00 / pack of 20

Which pack contains sausages at the lowest price each? ______

40) Singer, Kylie Star, received 5 fan letters in the post on Monday.

During the rest of the week the number of fan letters doubled every day.

How many letters did she receive on Friday? ______

END OF PAPER

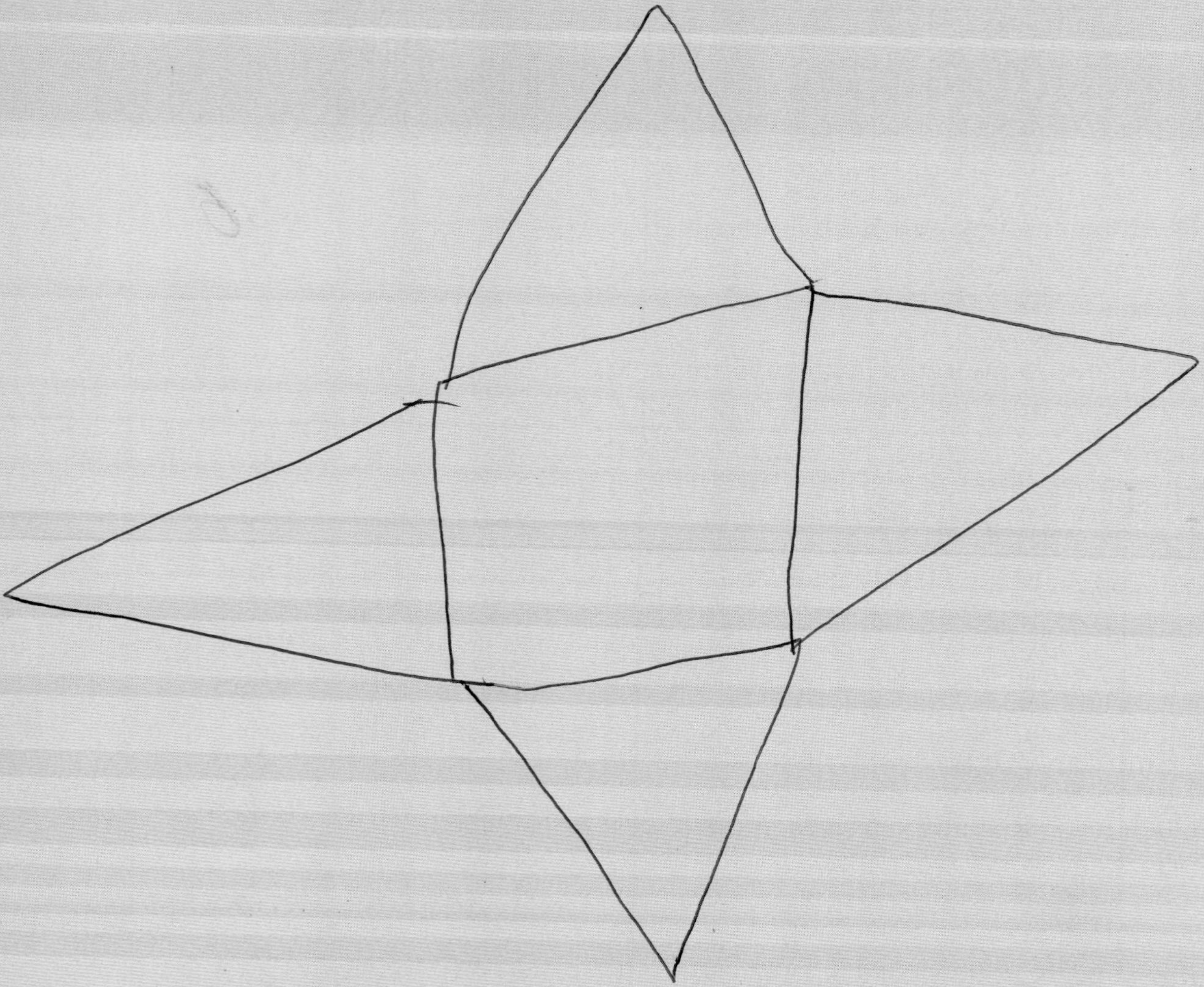

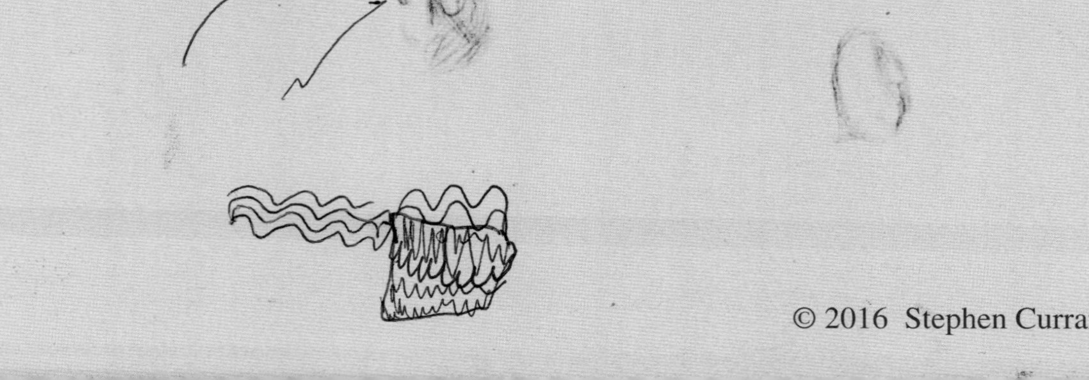

11+ Maths

Year 4/5

Testpack A

(GL Assessment Style)

Practice Papers 1-4

Answers and guidance notes for parents

These practice papers can be completed as standard or multiple-choice tests.

Multiple-choice Tests

Your child should mark their answers on the multiple-choice answer sheets. It is important for them to treat it like the real thing and record an answer in the appropriate box by drawing a clear line through their chosen box with a pencil. Clarity is important as the actual test would be marked by a computer. Mistakes should be carefully rubbed out and not crossed out since this would not be correctly recorded by the computer.

Standard Tests

Ask your child to fill in the answers in the spaces as instructed in each section. Mistakes should be crossed through with a single line and the correct answer written clearly.

Marking and Feedback

The answers are provided in this booklet. Only these answers are allowed. One mark should be given for each correct answer. Do not deduct marks for wrong answers. Do not allow half marks or 'benefit of the doubt', as this might mask a child's need for extra help in the topic and does not replicate the real exam conditions. Always try to be positive and encouraging. Talk through any mistakes with your child and work out together how to arrive at the correct answer.

Timing

Each test should take 40 minutes, however it is more important that a child completes the test accurately and does not rush. Children will speed up naturally with practice.

Score	%
1	3%
2	5%
3	8%
4	10%
5	13%
6	15%
7	18%
8	20%
9	23%
10	25%

Score	%
11	28%
12	30%
13	33%
14	35%
15	38%
16	40%
17	43%
18	45%
19	48%
20	50%

Score	%
21	53%
22	55%
23	58%
24	60%
25	63%
26	65%
27	68%
28	70%
29	73%
30	75%

Score	%
31	78%
32	80%
33	83%
34	85%
35	88%
36	90%
37	93%
38	95%
39	98%
40	100%

Answers

Practice Paper 1

1) A	11) 4,000	21) C	31) 15p
2) 5.6	12) 8	22) D	32) 30%
3) 5	13) C	23) A	33) D: (5, 4) C: (1, 2)
4) 50	14) 20	24) 13	34) 4
5) D	15) A & E	25) 76	35) 36%
6) 170	16) 40	26) C	36) £9.00
7) C	17) 18	27) $^1/_2$	37) C
8) A	18) 34	28) 46m	38) 88
9) E	19) 30p	29) A	39) 2hrs 45mins
10) 36	20) C	30) 16	40) £6.00

Practice Paper 2

1) 6 litres	11) 120	21) 42	31) 37
2) £1.75	12) B	22) A & E	32) B
3) 60%	13) $^1/_4$	23) 26 miles	33) 11.30
4) 13	14) 275	24) 20%	34) $40cm^2$
5) D	15) 81	25) 161,600	35) 40
6) 37p	16) 13	26) 12	36) 60p
7) 20	17) 44m	27) A	37) E
8) 8	18) B	28) $^1/_5$	38) E
9) 115°	19) D: (0, 4)	29) 16	39) £4.50
10) 9.97	20) 175	30) £8.70	40) 22

Answers

Practice Paper 3

1) 130m
2) $^{1}/_{3}$
3) 240
4) E
5) D
6) A
7) B
8) 16cm
9) 14p
10) 34
11) 44
12) 9.07
13) 4
14) 250g
15) 6
16) $^{3}/_{5}$
17) U: (5, 2)
    T: (1, 3)
18) 6
19) B
20) A
21) C
22) 188
23) D
24) B
25) 2hrs 15mins
26) £24.25
27) E
28) 80
29) 4,200
30) 15
31) E
32) 17
33) B
34) 18
35) 9
36) 10°C
37) E
38) 15
39) 200
40) $^{3}/_{8}$

Practice Paper 4

1) 8
2) 9
3) 150cm^3
4) $^{3}/_{8}$
5) 12
6) 17p
7) 64%
8) 120°
9) 300mℓ
10) 54m^2
11) 11
12) 5
13) $^{3}/_{5}$
14) 5
15) D: (6, 5)
    C: (5, 1)
16) 23°C
17) A
18) 360
19) £35
20) 13
21) 34
22) D
23) 14.0
24) 9cm^2
25) $^{2}/_{3}$
26) 100
27) $^{3}/_{7}$
28) 4.15pm
29) 2hrs 15mins
30) £4.80
31) B
32) 48
33) £47.00
34) 9
35) D
36) E
37) 380
38) £36
39) E
40) 80

PROGRESS CHARTS

Paper	Total Score	Percentage
Practice Paper 1	/ 40	%
Practice Paper 2	/ 40	%
Practice Paper 3	/ 40	%
Practice Paper 4	/ 40	%

Overall Percentage | % | **For the average add up % and divide by 4**

Multiple-choice Answer Sheets

11+ Maths Year 4/5 Testpack A Practice Paper 1

1	2	3	4	5	6	7
A	5.17	5	55	A	230	A
B	5.67	8	60	B	170	B
C	5.16	6	65	C	210	C
D	5.60	4	50	D	160	D
E	5.06	7	45	E	270	E

8	9	10	11	12	13	14
A	A	28	400	5	A	-20
B	B	44	40,000	8	B	11
C	C	16	2,200	7	C	16
D	D	36	4,000	9	D	20
E	E	27	220	6	E	27

15	16	17	18	19	20	21
A & E	180	15	38	30p	A	A
A & C	30	18	30	25p	B	B
B & C	60	21	36	12p	C	C
D & E	40	17	32	18p	D	D
C & E	360	24	34	40p	E	E

22	23	24	25	26	27	28
A	A	12	76	A	$\frac{3}{4}$	25m
B	B	9	38	B	$\frac{3}{6}$	40m
C	C	10	36	C	$\frac{3}{5}$	50m
D	D	15	32	D	$\frac{2}{3}$	46m
E	E	13	72	E	$\frac{1}{2}$	52m

29	30	31	32	33	34	35
A	13	15p	60%	D: (5, 4) C: (1, 2)	5	9%
B	18	22p	30%	D: (1, 2) C: (5, 4)	4	48%
C	15	20p	15%	D: (4, 5) C: (1, 2)	6	52%
D	16	10p	40%	D: (2, 1) C: (4, 5)	8	36%
E	14	16p	25%	D: (5, 4) C: (2, 1)	7	18%

36	37	38	39	40
£11.50	A	112	2hrs 45mins	£6.60
£18.00	B	64	120mins	£7.20
£9.00	C	92	2hrs 30mins	£6.00
£8.50	D	88	2hrs 50mins	£5.80
£10.50	E	76	3hrs 05mins	£4.80

1
- 8 litres
- 4 litres
- 6 litres
- 25 litres
- 16 litres

2
- £1.80
- £1.55
- £1.75
- £1.90
- £1.85

3
- 50%
- 80%
- 60%
- 40%
- 70%

4
- 15
- 13
- 17
- 14
- 16

5
- A
- B
- C
- D
- E

6
- 47p
- 39p
- 32p
- 37p
- 43p

7
- 20
- 22
- 15
- 18
- 25

8
- 8
- 5
- 9
- 7
- 6

9
- 110°
- 125°
- 105°
- 115°
- 120°

10
- 9.9
- 10.05
- 9.59
- 10.1
- 9.97

11
- 125
- 110
- 120
- 115
- 130

12
- A
- B
- C
- D
- E

13
- $\frac{1}{4}$
- $\frac{3}{8}$
- $\frac{2}{5}$
- $\frac{2}{8}$
- $\frac{1}{2}$

14
- 175
- 225
- 205
- 275
- 150

15
- 162
- 81
- 108
- 54
- 27

16
- 14
- 15
- 13
- 12
- 16

17
- 44m
- 25m
- 47m
- 100m
- 88m

18
- A
- B
- C
- D
- E

19
- (1, 5)
- (0, 4)
- (4, 1)
- (0, 5)
- (4, 0)

20
- 125
- 175
- 100
- 75
- 150

21
- 30
- 70
- 42
- 28
- 62

22
- A & C
- A & E
- B & E
- C & D
- C & E

23
- 20 miles
- 26 miles
- 16 miles
- 14 miles
- 52 miles

24
- 30%
- 25%
- 20%
- 15%
- 35%

25
- 161,700
- 161,000
- 161,750
- 161,600
- 161,500

26
- 15
- 9
- 12
- 10
- 14

27
- A
- B
- C
- D
- E

28
- $\frac{1}{4}$
- $\frac{3}{8}$
- $\frac{1}{5}$
- $\frac{2}{5}$
- $\frac{1}{2}$

29
- 16
- 18
- 12
- 20
- 14

30
- £7.80
- £8.70
- £7.90
- £8.30
- £9.10

31
- 35
- 33
- 27
- 30
- 37

32
- A
- B
- C
- D
- E

33
- 11.20
- 11.03
- 11.30
- 11.50
- 12.90

34
- $20cm^2$
- $100cm^2$
- $30cm^2$
- $40cm^2$
- $80cm^2$

35
- 20
- 24
- 40
- 36
- 32

36
- 60p
- 45p
- 50p
- 45p
- 30p

37
- A
- B
- C
- D
- E

38
- A
- B
- C
- D
- E

39
- £4.50
- £3.75
- £4.00
- £4.25
- £4.75

40
- 20
- 24
- 28
- 22
- 32

1
101m
130m
65m
95m
120m

2
$\frac{1}{4}$
$\frac{1}{3}$
$\frac{3}{8}$
$\frac{2}{6}$
$\frac{1}{2}$

3
210
200
240
180
220

4
A
B
C
D
E

5
A
B
C
D
E

6
A
B
C
D
E

7
A
B
C
D
E

8
14cm
16cm
18cm
13cm
17cm

9
15p
13p
20p
18p
14p

10
35
32
37
34
40

11
35
44
37
26
42

12
9.17
9.07
97.0
9.7
7.09

13
8
4
12
6
18

14
200g
500g
150g
250g
300g

15
4
6
7
5
3

16
$\frac{6}{10}$
$\frac{3}{8}$
$\frac{2}{5}$
$\frac{3}{5}$
$\frac{1}{4}$

17
U: (3, 1) T: (5, 2)
U: (5, 2) T: (1, 3)
U: (1, 3) T: (2, 5)
U: (2, 5) T: (1, 3)
U: (5, 2) T: (3, 1)

18
8
6
7
9
5

19
A
B
C
D
E

20
A
B
C
D
E

21
A
B
C
D
E

22
218
168
418
318
188

23
A
B
C
D
E

24
A
B
C
D
E

25
2hrs 45mins
3hrs 30mins
3hrs 15mins
2hrs 15mins
2hrs 30mins

26
£24.25
£36.20
£97.00
£28.50
£48.50

27
A
B
C
D
E

28
10
30
50
70
80

29
4,200
1,300
420
130
3,600

30
14
15
20
18
12

31
A
B
C
D
E

32
12
15
-12
17
-9

33
A
B
C
D
E

34
36
28
16
24
18

35
13
7
11
9
15

36
-13°C
10°C
17°C
-10°C
13°C

37
A
B
C
D
E

38
14
15
12
10
13

39
250
160
140
150
200

40
$\frac{5}{8}$
$\frac{1}{4}$
$\frac{2}{5}$
$\frac{1}{2}$
$\frac{3}{8}$

1
7
10
11
8
9

2
9
12
11
8
10

3
$110cm^3$
$300cm^3$
$180cm^3$
$150cm^3$
$200cm^3$

4
$^3/_8$
$^1/_3$
$^5/_8$
$^2/_3$
$^1/_4$

5
11
12
9
10
13

6
12p
15p
17p
19p
13p

7
36%
72%
68%
32%
64%

8
45°
120°
150°
90°
180°

9
3,000mℓ
0.03 litres
300cℓ
300mℓ
3cℓ

10
$45m^2$
$54m^2$
$72m^2$
$62m^2$
$58m^2$

11
8
12
10
9
11

12
10
8
9
13
5

13
$^3/_5$
$^1/_8$
$^3/_{10}$
$^3/_8$
$^2/_5$

14
5
8
7
4
6

15
D: (5, 1) C: (6, 5)
D: (5, 6) C: (5, 1)
D: (1, 5) C: (5, 6)
D: (6, 5) C: (5, 1)
D: (5, 6) C: (1, 5)

16
13°C
5°C
18°C
23°C
-5°C

17
A
B
C
D
E

18
120
360
180
160
240

19
£27
£45
£40
£35
£60

20
11
16
14
10
13

21
28
26
34
30
32

22
A
B
C
D
E

23
10.04
12.20
14.00
10.40
14.40

24
$12cm^2$
$9cm^2$
$14cm^2$
$10cm^2$
$8cm^2$

25
$^3/_4$
$^5/_8$
$^1/_2$
$^2/_3$
$^5/_6$

26
150
110
125
100
135

27
$^3/_8$
$^2/_3$
$^3/_4$
$^5/_8$
$^3/_7$

28
4.30am
16.45
4.15pm
17.15
4.45pm

29
2hrs 15mins
3hrs 10mins
2hrs 00mins
3hrs 15mins
2hrs 45mins

30
£4.00
£5.20
£4.60
£4.80
£4.40

31
A
B
C
D
E

32
38
26
18
56
48

33
£44.00
£45.50
£42.50
£56.50
£47.00

34
11
9
12
10
8

35
A
B
C
D
E

36
A
B
C
D
E

37
280
380
376
360
190

38
£36
£34
£40
£32
£30

39
A
B
C
D
E

40
105
80
155
125
75

CERTIFICATE OF

ACHIEVEMENT

This certifies

____

has successfully completed

11+ Maths

Year 4/5

TESTPACK **A** PAPERS **1-4**

Overall percentage score achieved ☐ %

Comment ____

____

Signed ____
(teacher/parent/guardian)

Date ____